Shakespeare's Amazing Traveling Adventure

Written by Nicoletta Barrie
Illustrations by Cassiopeia Medlock
Inspired by Karen Nolan

ISBN: 978-0692296127

Dedication

In Loving Memory

of

Our Shakespeare

From

"A Street Somewhere In Fairport, New York"
He was still new to the neighborhood,
and like a lot of cats, he was curious.

A percentage of every sale goes to Lollypop Farm

99 Victor Rd Fairport, NY 14450

(585) 223-1330 www.lollypop.org

Acknowledgements
Thank you all for
your talents Shaky

Nicoletta Barrie Author
Cassiopeia Medlock Author and
Illustrator of children's books

Mary K. Dougherty Book Publishing Coach for
16 years and service provider

Have your Pet's story or your own
Written, Illustrated Publish And Promoted At
Bootstrappublishing.net

mkd@bootstrappublishing.net
480-560-4933

Shakespeare's Amazing Traveling Adventure

Introduction

Shakespeare, a seven pound, black domestic short hair was already six years old when he was adopted into his forever home. He had been homeless and taken in by a family in Buffalo, New York. When they moved to Fairport, outside of Rochester, New York, Shakespeare was banished to the garage, which didn't suit him one bit. He wandered around the neighborhood until the Nolan family (mother, father, son and grandson) finally took him in. But did they really? What may be closer to the truth is that Shakespeare decided he liked it at the Nolans and so he stayed. He endeared himself to them and they, in turn, bonded with him over one very short summer. The Buffalo family was grateful when the Nolans took Shakespeare in because the cat spent most of his time there anyway.

Shakespeare liked to spread his charm around, however, and he made himself at home wherever he went. He often looked in on other families on the block and checked back in with his former companions from time to time too. He was friends with some of the wildlife in the neighborhood, including a white tailed deer and a den of foxes. He could knock on doors, liked to crash parties, used pet doors like they were made just for him, and if he got hungry in his excursions, he'd go fishing in a neighbors pond. He was a sociable animal, but once he decided the Nolans were his family, he always went home at night.

Some people on the block called Shakespeare the Mayor because he was present for every event, from barbecues to wedding receptions, to children's birthday parties. While he didn't shake anyone's hand like a politician (or even a dog) might, he did greet everyone with his golden eyes in a glance that seemed to see into their very souls. Anyone who spoke with Shakespeare would tell you that he hung onto every word, he was a great listener.

The Adventure Begins

One day in early autumn, Shakespeare walked up the ramp on a moving van to carry out one of his typical mayoral inspections. He weaved in and out of the boxes and furniture in the van, and when he was tired of looking around, he stretched and yawned and, like cats sometimes do, decided it was time for a nap. Shakespeare fell fast asleep on top of an armoire, the highest spot in the van.

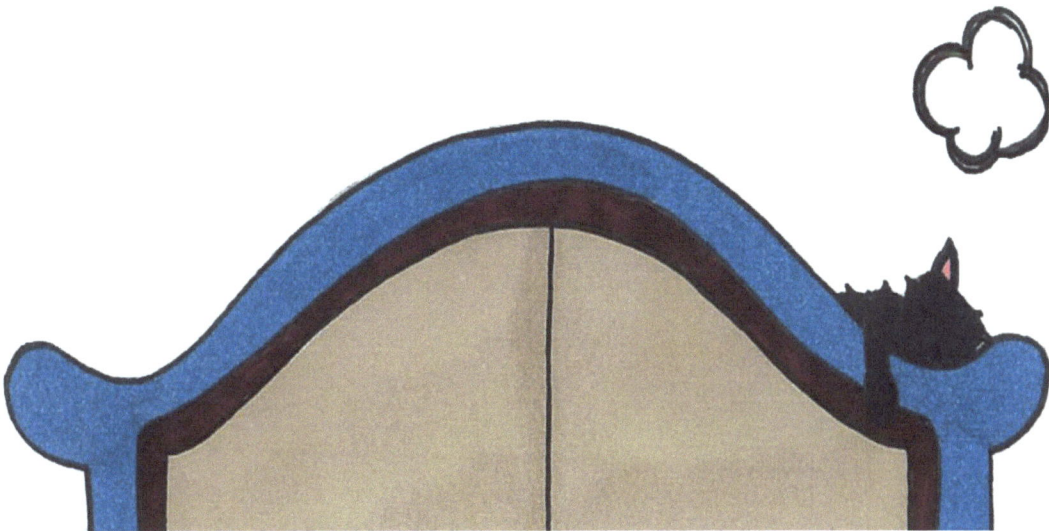

While dreaming of serenading the female cat next door from her backyard fence, Shakespeare was jarred awake as the van doors closed out the afternoon night.

Shakespeare cried, a long drawn out croaking that was more like a toad than a cat. "Muroowl! Muroowl!" The sound was loud and soulful, no one heard it. The van begins to move.

Cats can see in the dark as long as the dark is not absolute. They have a special layer if cells at the back of their retinas that act like a mirror, reflecting light back to the retina's cells. So in near darkness, cats eyes collect what light there is and give the retina a second chance to absorb it.

Shakespeare could not only see inside the van, but he could also use his twenty or so long whiskers as sensory devices to avoid running into all of the household items that had been carefully and closely packed inside. He looked around for an exit, any exit even a small hole in the floor that would do. Shakespeare was small; the best he could find was a crack on one side of the van. He could watch trees go by, but it was far too narrow to allow him to slip out. Besides, they were moving pretty fast down the highway. Not being a nervous Nelly, Shakespeare settled down and began to preen.

The trip wasn't long. The ride was fast and smooth enough that nothing inside the van slid or fell down. Shakespeare had ridden in cars enough to know that the slow, short spurts of speed and squeaky brake sounds meant city driving and stops for traffic lights. Once out of the city, the cars moved faster and stopped less.

Yearning for Home

When the van came to a stop and the engine was turned off, Shakespeare stretched as he listened to one cab door close and then the other. Shakespeare prepared to take action when the van was opened up again.

It was seconds, the heavy metal doors swung out and the golden light of the late afternoon poured in the van. Shakespeare bolted, skimming over the hair on one mover's head as he raced his way to the ground, anxious to shake the experience off of himself and take a look at his captors. They looked back, stunned to see that this beautiful black cat had been inside their van.

Shakespeare didn't hang around; he turned and ran in the direction of his home. That is, it would have been in that direction had the van stopped at the exact same spot where Shakespeare got on. The van was now in Baldwinsville, just outside of Syracuse, some 70 miles from Shakespeare's home in Fairport.

We've all heard stories about lost cats finding their way home from long distances. They're likely true, it happens. Yet, the sad reality is that just as many don't find their way. Those who manage to find their way home use their senses to guide them, and those senses are powerful.

Cats have 19 million scent-receptive nerve endings in their noses, compared to 5 million in humans, making their sense of smell keener than that of humans. They can hear sounds two octaves higher than what we hear; they may even perceive sounds from all sides, which is a help in orienting themselves. Their eyesight is more acute than humans; their pupils can dilate wider. One study found that cats can even resort to flashes of memory of audio and visual images to replay in their heads. Every whisker and every hair in a cats coat receives information and sends it to the brain. Perhaps most incredible of all, studies currently are being conducted to determine of cats, like migratory birds, can naturally detect the earth's gravitational field, giving them a sense of direction even without visual cues. Lastly, they have a strong homing instinct.

It didn't take long for Shakespeare to realize that his neighborhood was gone. This place smelled different, it looked different, it felt different. It was nice enough, but Shakespeare loved his family, his neighbors, even the mailman and delivery guys that came down the street every day and sometimes brought him treats. He would just have to find his way home.

Shakespeare began his trek to return to the Nolans, opening himself up to all of the sounds, smells and sights around him and to the feeling that instinctive urge to turn this way or that.

Shakespeare walked a couple of miles through the residential neighborhood into an active shopping district where the aroma of salmon wafted to his nose from a restaurant named Turbot. Shakespeare didn't see a doorbell so he tried to open the front door by pressing his nose against it real hard and then releasing it, but that method, so useful on the inside doors back home didn't work here. When a man came out and stomped his feet at Shakespeare, saying "Shoo, shoo!" Shakespeare decided to find the alley and go dumpster diving instead.

Danger awaited Shakespeare in the alley. He no sooner reached Turbot's dumpster when a Labrador retriever spotted him and began a chase. Because his stomach was empty, Shakespeare took a risk he might not have otherwise taken. He ran down the alley, and then turned to stare at the Labrador. Shocked and maybe a little afraid the Labrador stopped dead in her tracks. Then, before she could process what was happening, Shakespeare started running directly towards her, took a flying leap and dove directly into the dumpster. This was dumpster diving at its most literal.

Shakespeare landed in a slippery mess, but his nose detected odors that were fresh and wholesome. Shakespeare enjoyed a meal of salmon and white sauce, the Labrador jumped straight up in the air trying to get a look at the feast she was missing. Shakespeare was done—even though this wasn't the ideal place to take a nap, he decided to wait out the Labrador and curled up in a reasonably clean empty box.

Catching a Ride

It seems as though Shakespeare was fated to waking up in difficult situations. The first time was the moving van, this time it was a garbage truck. The truck grabbed hold of the dumpster, lifted it and just as the trash was falling into the hopper, Shakespeare collected himself and shot to the top of the truck like a rocket.

Shakespeare could have jumped down from the truck. It was headed in the general direction of his home however, and so he took advantage of that by hitching a ride. He held on, sometimes unsteadily, while the truck made numerous stops to pick up more trash before heading out to the dump site that was on the outskirts of town. Once there, Shakespeare jumped off and headed towards the woods while shaking off the distasteful smells and uncomfortable ride of the dumpster.

Shakespeare trudged through mud and brush. He climbed small hills and walked around ponds. He found shelter when it rained and basked in the sun after a cold night, days passed.

While trekking the Montezuma Wetlands Complex, he came across a wild turkey. He had never seen a wild turkey before, only the farm raised, in a burst of noise and chaos, and the coyote turned his attention towards Shakespeare. The coyote was fast and Shakespeare lost a little ground every time he turned to see how close the coyote actually was. Finally, Shakespeare ran up a tree. Fortunately, none of Shakespeare's companions had him declawed, so he was able to move fast and efficiently.

Coyotes can climb trees too however, and this one started to, but Shakespeare didn't stop until he reached the top of the 25 foot beechwood. That was too high for him. So this coyote backed down and returned to hunting turkeys or some other prey that wasn't as fast as Shakespeare. Shakespeare rested in the beechwood treetop for a while as the chaos took a lot out of him. At dusk, he descended and at the base of the tree, Shakespeare was met by a doe and her fawn.

The deer were grazing, but it was almost like they were waiting for Shakespeare. They cautiously approached each other and touched noses. Feeling comfortable together, the deer led Shakespeare into deep cover. They located a suitable spot and pressed down vegetation with their bodies to make a bed. They huddled together to share body warmth.

Deer never sleep in the same bed twice, deterring predators from catching their scent. They sleep in short spurts and are alert to any movement in their surroundings. Their tails are designed to flip up, showing their white undersides which warn other in their group of approaching danger.

Shakespeare felt safe with the doe and her fawn. Even though he preferred meat, being a carnivore, he grazed on vegetation with them (deer are herbivores) and gained strength for the next part of his journey.

Shakespeare enjoyed the company of the deer, but after awhile he yearned for more creature comforts, like sleeping inside. He noticed that the nights were getting colder. All sorts of pricker bushes and little insects critters kept getting stuck in his fur, causing him to spend hours grooming. The deer were like superheroes to him with their ability to detect and evade predators, but always having to think about predators was difficult for Shakespeare.

He had been homeless once, and he knew how cruel that life could be.

He had a nice warm home waiting for him, and he wanted to get back to it. Many days had passed since Shakespeare had seen his family and he missed them.

Shakespeare readied himself to continue on his journey. The deer accompanied Shakespeare from the Wetlands through wooded areas around Galen and Lyons and Newark before they touched noses as though to say goodbye and then headed back to Montezuma.

Shakespeare was on his own again, but he sensed that he wasn't far from home. In fact, he was less than 13 miles away. He picked up his pace along Route 31, more anxious than ever to see his family again.

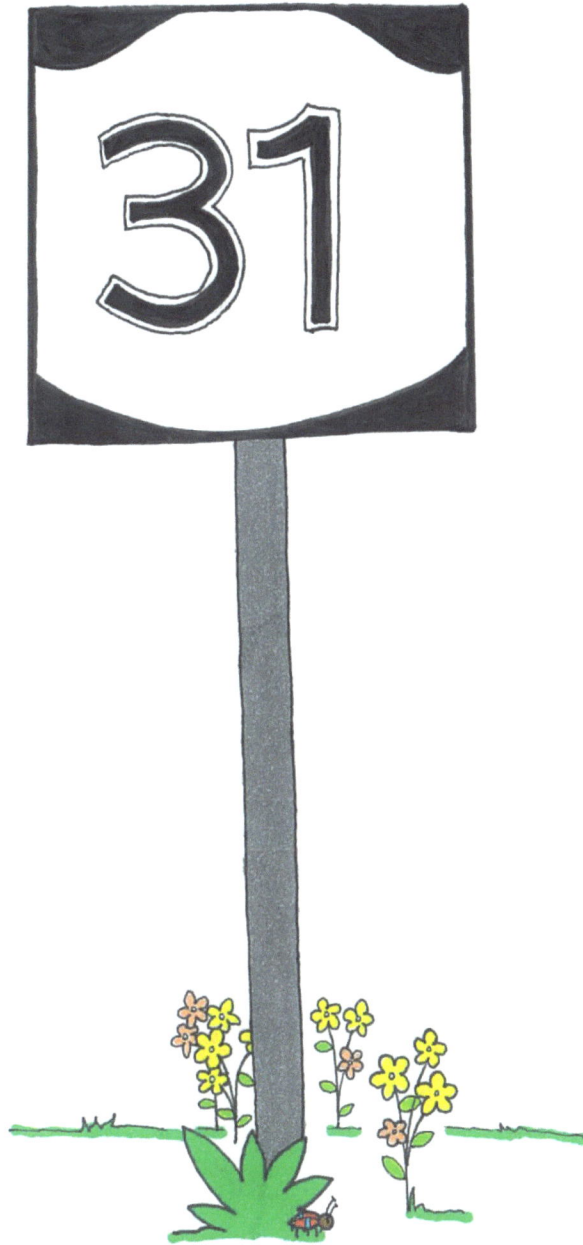

The Search

The movers called the Nolans the day after the move. It took that long for their clients to figure out the cat had to be Shakespeare, The Mayor, who was always getting into mischief. The Nolans were beside themselves with worry when Shakespeare didn't come home the night before, and they took some relief in at least knowing what had happened. Now they had to figure out how to find Shakespeare and bring him home.

That weekend Mr. and Mrs. Nolan and their son Peter drove to the address on Baldwinsville that the movers gave them. They walked door to door with a photograph of Shakespeare and retraced his journey through the neighborhood. They contacted local animal rescue groups and animal control, but none of the leads turned out to have anything to do with Shakespeare. They put up posters with Shakespeare's picture and their cell phone number and a few calls came with good information.

From these calls, they discovered that Shakespeare was headed in the right direction, the direction of home. Would he be able to make it all the way? They couldn't take that chance. Because of work and school, they could only look for him on weekends.

The following weekend, the Nolans drove to Baldwinsville again. This time, they concentrated on a small business district in the vicinity where Shakespeare was last seen. The first person they spoke with was a sales clerk who worked in a fabric store. She had called them during the week to say she saw Shakespeare sitting on a park bench like he was waiting for a bus. "Do you think he could have gotten on a bus?" she asked. It was easy to check this out by calling the bus company, whose receptionist was happy to help. She had the driver on that route for that day call the Nolans. While he remembered a beautiful black cat sitting on a park bench, he said that the cat didn't get in his bus despite some children calling "kitty, kitty, kitty" and trying to lure him with popcorn and other snacks.

The cat sat on his haunches, the driver said, and seemed to wave to the kids. "Strangest thing I ever saw a cat do." said the driver. "Fact is, if he had gotten on the bus, I probably would have taken him home with me."

This news gave the Nolans confirmation that Shakespeare was alive and well and as sociable as ever.

The Nolans continued to search this shopping area and talk with the shopkeepers some who had seen Shakespeare and told stories of how friendly he was and unafraid of them. One man commented on how Shakespeare looked him right in the eye when he talked to the cat. Another marveled at how after a brief rainstorm, Shakespeare avoided walking through any puddles yet still shook off his dry feet as though they were wet. A renter in the area told them that Shakespeare had climbed up the fire escape ladder to her apartment and stared at her through her kitchen window. "So sweet," she said. "I couldn't resist giving him some ham and milk."

Their last stop of the day was at Turbot, where they also had an early dinner before heading home. The chef there told them that Shakespeare had been spotted sleeping in a dumpster out back, just before the garbage pickup. He feared their cat may have been picked up by garbage men. The Nolans used their smart phone to look up the location of the Baldwinsville garbage dump.

The dump was conveniently located on their route back home. They got permission to look anywhere in the outer region of the dump, but they were not allowed to go through the piles of garbage. Right away, Peter found a bell he thought might have come off of Shakespeare's collar; it sure looked like the same bell.

They continued to search in that area and found what looked like a tiny paw prints in the dried mud.

The Nolans were not confident that the paw prints were Shakespeare's. Even the bell was questionable, but still these discoveries offered them hope.

Nearly half way home, the Nolans decided to get off the New York State Thruway and take a more scenic route back to Fairport. They were all exhausted from their search for Shakespeare and sad to be going home without him yet again. Once on Route 31 near Lyons, Peter spotted a white tailed deer and her yearling. "Look" he said. The Nolans slowed down to look at the beautiful animals and the deer stopped and looked at them. The Nolans and the deer both seemed to recognize something familiar in the other in the brief moment they locked eyes. The white tails went up and the deer bounded away.

Little did they know just how close they were to Shakespeare in that moment.

Then the Nolans went to bed that night, they were a little sadder, had a little less hope and were dead tired. The house seemed so empty without Shakespeare. They could feel his absence in every corner.

Morning After

Peter woke up first, he felt a little better than the night before, a little more hopeful about Shakespeare. He showered and got dressed and when he went downstairs to the kitchen, Mrs. Nolan too was up and had poured him a glass of orange juice and put cereal milk and bowls on the table. They heard Mr. Nolans footsteps on the stairs.

"I don't believe it!" shouted Mr. Nolan, "get out here you two!" Mrs. Nolan and Peter ran to the stairs just as Mr. Nolan was opening the front door.

They heard him first "Muroowl! Muroowl!" Dare they believe it? Could that be Shakespeare? They couldn't get out that door quick enough. There stood Shakespeare, golden eyes looking up at them, a little worse for wear, but home again, reunited with the best family The Mayor could ever want.

A Most Sociable Cat

I had no say in the matter; he just walked into my life and took over a big part of my every day pursuits. Whether I was outside gardening, washing the car, or sitting on the porch reading, he came over, and parked himself next to me and proceeded to give me the adult supervision he deemed I required. If I was inside, he would come up on the porch bench and very persistently bang on the window with his front paw until I surrendered and came out to sit on the bench with him to scratchy his ears and while I gave him a few small treats.

His name was Shakespeare, a rather small sized almost totally deaf black cat, he liked dogs (he had been raised with them) was anything but aloof (as most people claim cats to be)and was, in fact, the most cordial, affable and congenial creature any of us had ever seen. It wasn't that he overdid any of this; he had gravitas, a real presence that said he knew his worth and had no need to prove it to anyone.

That's not to say that he didn't have minor faults but they only served to endear him to us all the more. He fancied himself a hunter! He would capture chipmunks in my backyard and stroll around with them alive carrying them gently in his mouth to display them to us until I'd catch hold of his tail, remove and release them. I never had to fear that he might bite or scratch. He never did!

When the deer herd came up put of the woods into the backyard (they knew it was safe refuge) He would stalk them much to their curious amusement. There he would be, belly scraping the ground, slow-motion creeping like a lion stalking a springbok on the Serengeti, until he was almost nose to nose. At the very last moment he would spring away, and saunter off as if he had carried the day and saved the yard!

Each day he visited all of us in turn, making his rounds in a calm, stately manner and bringing a special warmth and camaraderie with him. On special occasions such as summer weddings or graduations that were celebrated outdoors he would be among the first to arrive and the last to leave and always a welcome quest. Whether he was catching goldfish from my ponds. Inspecting our garages (If they were open they were meticulously inspected) or supervising my setting put Halloween decorations, he was a wonderful part of all our lives.

He's gone now, but a little bit of him lives on in each of us.

Ted

A Word From Shakespeare

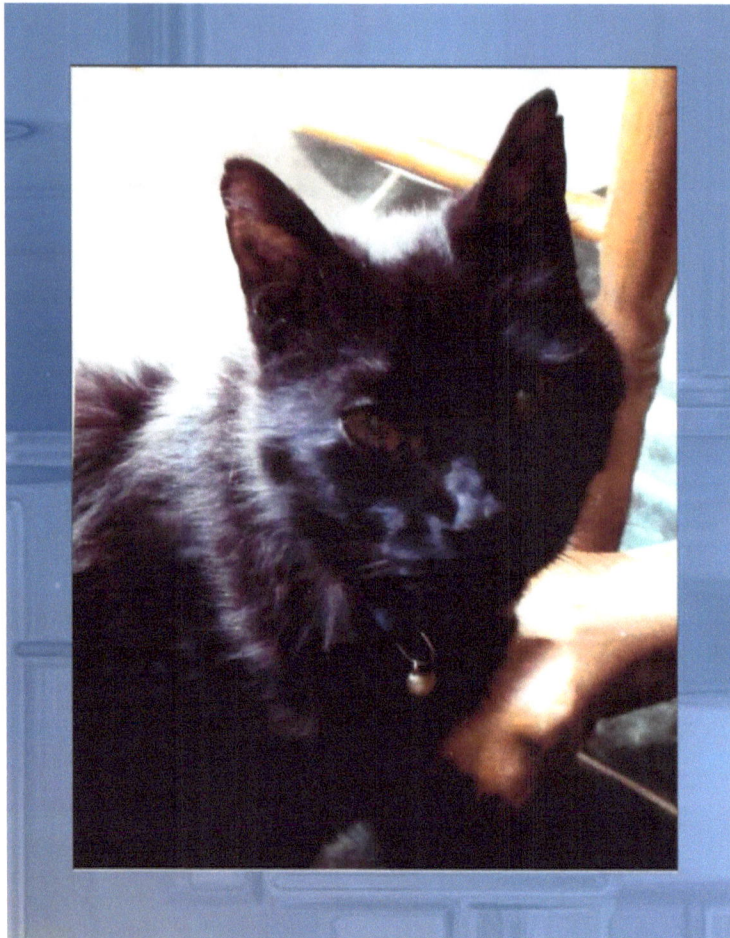

1. I would like to say thank you to my new neighborhood for your kindness and in welcoming me.

2. I would like to say thank you to my mommy Katie for rescuing me and bringing me here to Fairport, loving me and calling me your "shake and bake".

3. I would like to say thank you to my daddy peter for loving me no matter what, taking good care of me and calling me "pookie"

www.ingramcontent.com/pod-product-compliance
Lightning Source LLC
Chambersburg PA
CBHW041427090426

42741CB00002B/74